The Great Journey
to Scotland

福田範子／福田剛士〈著〉

二瓶社

Contents

Unit 1 5
    Scene 1   チェックイン
    Scene 2   保安検査

Unit 2 11
    Scene 1   出国審査と搭乗
    Scene 2   離陸

Unit 3 17
    Scene 1   ロングフライト（1）
    Scene 2   ロングフライト（2）

Unit 4 23
    Scene 1   乗り継ぎ地での入国審査
    Scene 2   アムステルダムでの朝食

Unit 5 29
    Scene 1   グラスゴーへのフライト
    Scene 2   グラスゴーのホテルに到着

Unit 6 35
    Scene 1   夕食の買い出し
    Scene 2   グラスゴーでのディナー

Unit 7 41
    Scene 1   いざ、エディンバラへ！
    Scene 2   観光都市エディンバラ

Unit 8 47
    Scene 1   国立スコットランド美術館
    Scene 2   パブでのランチ

Unit 9 53
    Scene 1　エディンバラ城
    Scene 2　要塞を巡る（1）

Unit 10 59
    Scene 1　要塞を巡る（2）
    Scene 2　スコッチウィスキー・エクスペリエンス（1）

Unit 11 65
    Scene 1　スコッチウィスキー・エクスペリエンス（2）
    Scene 2　カフェで一休み

Unit 12 73
    Scene 1　プロバンド領主館
    Scene 2　ケルヴィングローヴ美術館＆博物館

Unit 13 79
    Scene 1　はく製標本
    Scene 2　ダリとミレーの絵画

Unit 14 85
    Scene 1　ブキャナンストリート
    Scene 2　クィーンストリート

Unit 15 91
    Scene 1　グラスゴー空港へ
    Scene 2　離陸

Unit 16 95
    Scene 1　日本へのロングフライト
    Scene 2　帰国

Unit 1

■ Vocabulary Study: Scene 1

1. common （　）　a. リムジンバス
2. limousine bus （　）　b. 国際線の空港
3. international airport （　）　c. 共通の
4. terminal （　）　d. 旅券
5. sea breeze （　）　e. 海風
6. airline （　）　f. 発着ロビー
7. passport （　）　g. 航空会社

■ Vocabulary Study: Scene 2

1. security inspection （　）　a. 通貨の換金
2. currency exchange （　）　b. X線
3. baggage （　）　c. 保安検査
4. X-ray （　）　d. 手荷物
5. metal detector （　）　e. 可燃性の
6. trash box （　）　f. 金属探知器
7. flammable （　）　g. ゴミ箱（イギリス英語）
8. rubbish bin （　）　h. ゴミ箱（アメリカ英語）

Scene 1: Check in

Atsushi and Kojiro were classmates at university. They got along with each other because they had a common dream for the future. They wanted to work in foreign countries. During their school days, for the purpose of experiencing different culture, they planned to travel to Scotland. They could hardly wait for their summer vacation.

It was the middle of August. Expecting a crowd, Atsushi and Kojiro left home early. Atsushi arranged to meet Kojiro at the limousine bus stop in Nishinomiya. They were waiting impatiently for the Kansai International Airport-bound limousine bus. The summer heat made them slightly sweaty. Except for a young woman in a one-piece outfit, nobody was waiting for the bus.

Atsushi took part in a homestay programme in Hawaii when he was a high school student. That was why he often talked knowledgeably about travelling abroad. Kojiro was a slim and tall man who was kind enough to listen to Atsushi with a smile on his lips. For Kojiro it was the first time travelling abroad. The limousine bus came to the bus stop on time.

Kansai International Airport was opened on an artificial island in the sea of Izumisano in 1994. When the bus arrived at terminal 1 of the airport, Atsushi and Kojiro said, "Thank you" to the driver and got off the bus. Feeling the sea breeze, they entered terminal 1. For a moment, Kojiro said, "How wide the building is!" The check-in counters of the airlines are side by side, and they could not see the far end of the floor. In spite of it being early morning, terminal 1 is crowded.

■ **Dialogue**

Kojiro   "What do we have to do now?"
Atsushi   "First of all, we will check in at the airline counter. We need to

	show our tickets and passports"
Kojiro	"Is that all?"
Atsushi	"No, we check in our suitcases."
Kojiro	"OK! Which airline do we use? There are lots of airline counters. Do we use JAL? Or ANA?"
Atsushi	"No, we use KLM airline. Where is the KLM counter?"
Kojiro	"I found an information desk. Let's ask there."

■ 本文の内容に合うように、質問に答えなさい。

1．空港に到着したら、アツシとコジロウはまずどこへ行かなければならないか。
　_____

2．アツシとコジロウは、航空会社のカウンターで何をするか。
　_____

3．アツシとコジロウは、どの航空会社でチェックインをするか。
　_____

Scene 2: Security Inspection

Atsushi and Kojiro showed their student identification cards and took advantage of the student discount at the currency exchange. "What do we do next?" Kojiro asked Atsushi. "We have to go through a security inspection." Atsushi replied to him nervously.

 We need to go through the departure formalities when we leave our country. Before that, our baggage must be inspected using an X-ray system. In addition, the baggage owner has to be inspected with a metal detector. It's forbidden to carry on dangerous substances. Somehow, Atsushi had once been caught by a detector. Meanwhile, this was the first time for Kojiro. He didn't know what Atsushi was worried about.

 Atsushi was not hungry yet. However, Kojiro was hungry and he was fascinated by a nearby cafe. Kojiro's hunger was ignored by Atsushi, and they went directly to the security inspection area. Atsushi found many people lined up there. Atsushi looked at various trash boxes beside them. There were boxes for flammable trash and nonflammable trash, and also boxes for dangerous substances, such as knives and gas lighters. Atsushi said, with a knowing look, "British people don't use the word, 'trash box', but call it a 'rubbish bin.' " When Kojiro said "Why is that?", he replied " 'Trash box' is an American English term, and British people prefer the British term, 'rubbish bin.' "

 In the security inspection area, the inspectors were checking passports and boarding passes. Though the inspectors didn't hurry passengers, they put their baggage on the trays quickly. Atsushi and Kojiro put their watches, and digital cameras on trays. One inspector urged Kojiro to take off his jacket. When Kojiro had finished his check, he heard a buzzer from behind him. Kojiro turned back and found out that Atsushi was being body searched by the inspector. Kojiro said, "What's wrong?" Atsushi replied, "I forgot to take a pedometer out of my pocket."

【Notes】departure formalities: 出国審査 , body search: ボディーチェック , pedometer: 万歩計

Unit 1

■ 本文の内容と一致しているものはどれか。

1．（a）アツシが換金をする時、学生証がないので割引されなかった。
　　（b）アツシとコジロウは、空港についてすぐに朝食をとった。
　　（c）アツシとコジロウは、チェックインをした後、すぐに保安検査場に向かった。

2．（a）アツシは、保安検査場でリラックスしていた。
　　（b）アツシは、お腹が空いていた。
　　（c）アツシのところで、金属探知器のブザーが鳴った。

3．（a）コジロウが、飛行機に乗るのは数年ぶりであった。
　　（b）ライターを機内に持ち込むことは禁止されている。
　　（c）乗客は手荷物検査の際、皆リラックスしていた。

4．（a）検査官は、急ぐように指示を出していた。
　　（b）コジロウは金属探知器に引っ掛かった。
　　（c）アツシは、万歩計をポケットに入れたままだったので、ボディーチェックを受けた。

● コラム【換金とは？　英語と米語は違う！】

①換金について
　当然のことだが、原則海外では日本の通貨は使えない。クレジットカードが普及しているとはいえ、バスや電車での移動や小さい店での買い物の際に、クレジットカードが使えないこともある。そのため、滞在する国の通貨をある程度持っておく必要がある。現地に着いてからでも換金は可能だが、日本国内の空港で換金するのが一番お得であるといわれている。空港内の銀行によっても換金レートが異なり、学生割引をしてくれる所もあるので、銀行を比較してから、どこで換金するか決めることをお勧めする。

②イギリス英語とアメリカ英語の違いについて
　アメリカ合衆国では、ファストフード店で食べ物を持ち帰る際"Take out, please."と伝えるが、イギリスやイギリス圏の国へ行けば、けげんな顔をされて、"Take away?"と聞き直されてしまう。本文でアツシが"trash box"を"rubbish bin"と得意気に話すくだりがあるが、イギリスとアメリカでは、使用する単語が異なることがある。

Unit 2

■ Vocabulary Study: Scene 1

1. duty-free shop   (　)　　a. 通路
2. boarding   (　)　　b. 乗客
3. souvenir shop   (　)　　c. 搭乗
4. free shuttle   (　)　　d. 免税店
5. passenger   (　)　　e. 無料シャトル
6. aisle   (　)　　f. 土産物屋

■ Vocabulary Study: Scene 2

1. captain   (　)　　a. 流暢な
2. fluent   (　)　　b. 機内エンターテイメント
3. in-flight entertainment (　)　　c. 機長
4. cabin attendant   (　)　　d. 救命胴衣
5. life jacket   (　)　　e. 滑走路
6. emergency   (　)　　f. 客室乗務員
7. runway   (　)　　g. 緊急事態

Scene 1: Departure Formalities and Boarding

Atsushi and Kojiro passed the security inspection area, and then they took an escalator to go through the departure formalities. On the lower floor, there were many gates of inspection booths. If they went beyond the booths, it meant that they were abroad.

"Next person, please." One male inspector wearing glasses urged Kojiro. "Good morning." Kojiro greeted him with a nervous look and handed over his passport and his air ticket. The inspector looked at Kojiro seriously and checked his documents. The inspector put a stamp on his passport quietly and his passport and his air ticket were given back to Kojiro.

Atsushi was waiting for Kojiro beyond the inspection booth. "OK, Let's go!" "Yeah!" Kojiro looked with curiosity at the stores of Gucci and Chanel. After the departure formalities, the two young men felt hungry. However, there were only duty-free shops and souvenir shops, and they couldn't find cafes or restaurants. They had no choice but to go to the boarding gate, using a free shuttle.

They reached the boarding gate 30 minutes before boarding. At a waiting area, Atsushi stood up and started stretching. Atsushi said, "On the flight, we can hardly move our bodies freely like this." Kojiro accepted his suggestion and imitated Atsushi's stretching.

First, they heard the announcement of boarding for business class passengers. They listened attentively for a short while, and then they heard the announcement for economy class passengers.

Kojiro said, "Shall we go now?" "Wait a moment." Atsushi stopped him. Soon after the announcement, many of the passengers made a long line at the boarding gate. The staff repeated the same announcement twice. Atsushi stood up and urged Kojiro to go ahead for boarding, and they went to the gate. Atsushi found the newspaper rack in front of the door of the plane, and he got one of the Japanese newspapers. "Ohayougozaimasu," said a blue-eyed blonde cabin attendant to them. Inside the plane, there were three seats by the window at each side, and four seats in the middle of the plane. Atsushi and Kojiro's seats were at the rear area of the plane. They finally arrived at their seats. "These are special seats on the plane. There is much more space at the aisles" Atsushi said. "The cost of booking these seats is comparatively high, but my father paid the additional cost for us." "I want to say thank you to your father." Kojiro replied.

■ 本文の内容に合うように、質問に答えなさい。

1．出国審査では、何を提示しなくてはならないか。

_____

2．搭乗するまでの30分間、アツシとコジロウはどのように過ごしたか。

_____

3．アツシとコジロウの席は、機体のどのあたりにあったか。

_____

4．アツシとコジロウの席は、どういうスタイルか。

_____

Scene 2: Take off

Atsushi took out two small cushions from his baggage. He set them on each seat, "We will have pain on our hips with a long flight," he said. "Oh, I see. This flight is about twelve hours." Kojiro smiled and put on his slippers. Next, in the lavatory one after the other they changed out of their jeans and into soft jersey pants. Atsushi sat down at the window side and Kojiro sat down at the aisle side. Getting the valuable two seats, Atsushi talked, without pausing for breath about their lucky situation. Listening to Atsushi, Kojiro took a journal from the seat pocket.

Nowadays, in most flights, we can enjoy in-flight entertainment. The B5 size monitor is set up and you can enjoy music and movies. Atsushi tried to start the movie, but he could not start it until the plane took off.

There was a clear announcement saying that all passengers had boarded the plane. Atsushi and Kojiro heard the fluent English and they realised that they were travelling abroad. After that, there was the same announcement in Japanese. Next the captain greeted and explained the flight plan. On each aisle, cabin attendants explained how to use the life jacket and showed the escape process for an emergency. Atsushi and Kojiro checked their seat belts again. The big plane taxied to the runway. There was a short silence. Finally, the plane taxied down the runway with a thundering sound and the passengers were pressed to their seats by the gravity of acceleration. Then, they felt the smooth takeoff. The two young men looked at each other and smiled unconsciously. After a few minutes, Atsushi shouted, "I can't see the airport any more!" Kojiro looked out from the small window and found the sea of Kishu. A large ship seemed a little dot.

Unit 2

■ 本文の内容に合うものには○を、合わないものには×をつけなさい。
1. 長時間のフライト用に、座布団が備え付けられていた。
2. 機内エンターテイメントは、つまらないものが多かった。
3. 流暢な英語のアナウンスが流れた。
4. 機長による救命胴衣の説明があった。

● **コラム【長距離フライトの必需品】**

　長距離フライトでは、薄手の座布団やスリッパ、締め付けないズボンが大変役に立つ。座布団で腰やお尻が痛くならないようにすることも大事であり、ゆったりとくつろげる柔らかいズボンに着替えて、足を締め付けないようスリッパに履き替えることが望ましい。また、機内は空気が乾燥しているので、睡眠時にマスクをすることをお勧めしたい。これだけそろえれば、快適な空の旅を楽しめる。

Unit 3

■ Vocabulary Study: Scene 1

1. non-release movie （ ）　　a．おしぼり
2. moist hand towel （ ）　　b．ごちそう
3. feast （ ）　　c．封切り前の映画

■ Vocabulary Study: Scene 2

1. lavatory （ ）　　a．あくび
2. air cushion （ ）　　b．お手洗い
3. yawn （ ）　　c．空気枕
4. be sound asleep （ ）　　d．熟睡している

Scene 1: Long Flight (1)

There was an electronic sound, and the seatbelt sign was turned off. Some passengers stood up and took out their personal belongings from the baggage space below the ceiling. Atsushi tried to operate the monitor again.

"Wow! I found the non-release movies!" Atsushi was excited. Kojiro nodded and said, "We can see lots of Japanese movies." Atsushi selected a new Hollywood action movie. Kojiro started to enjoy a Japanese samurai movie.

After a short time, a blue-eyed blonde cabin attendant came and handed out moist hand towels for the passengers. Then, she pushed a cart which was full of beverages, such as juice, tea, beer and whisky. She asked the passengers in turn, "Anything to drink?" Atsushi ordered a glass of apple juice and Kojiro selected a glass of Coke. In addition, they were given an original KLM snack. Kojiro had a snack along with his drink. Next, lunch time started. The same cabin attendant pushed a cart along and asked them, "Japanese style or Western style?" Atsushi chose the Western style menu and Kojiro selected the Japanese style menu. Each menu had different dishes. The Western style option was hot chicken chop, fried potato, vegetable salad, and a piece of cake. On the other hand, the Japanese style plate had rice with soboro-meat, scrambled egg, and grilled salmon with salt. Soumen with shrimp and anmitsu were also on a plate. In addition, both plates had a bottle of water, a piece of bread, butter and jam. Their plates were a feast. In high spirits, Atsushi and Kojiro started lunch in the sky.

■ 本文の内容に合うように、質問に答えなさい。

1．アツシとコジロウは、機内エンターテイメントで何を楽しんだか。

_____

2．アツシとコジロウは、ドリンクのサービスで何を注文したか。

_____

3．ジャパニーズスタイルの機内食のデザートは何だったか。

Scene 2: Long Flight (2)

After eating lunch, Atsushi and Kojiro went to the lavatory one after the other. Fortunately, the lavatories were not crowded, so they could have time to brush their teeth. Atsushi blew up an air cushion, and fixed it around his neck. Atsushi said, "I'm sleepy." He gave big yawns again and again. He put on a mask and fell asleep easily. The lights were turned off in the plane. Kojiro was under the illusion that it was around midnight. He still wanted to enjoy the samurai movie, so he restarted the movie in the dark.

Atsushi was sound asleep. Kojiro was only half conscious, so he decided to stop the movie program. Most passengers were already sleeping. He turned off the monitor and closed his eyes. He thought, though, that he wouldn't go to sleep yet. He put on a pair of earphones and selected the relaxation music. There was healing music like the sound of waves, but he didn't like the tender music. He chose jazz and listened to it on the lowest volume. He was slowly falling asleep.

With a cheerful sound, the lights were turned on in succession. The pleasant aroma of coffee was in the air. Kojiro woke up and took off a pair of earphones. Atsushi and other passengers were beginning to wake up. They were provided with light meals.

The two young men had scrambled eggs, a piece of bread and a dessert. The captain's announcement raised their spirits, because he informed that there was only 1 hour before they would get to the airport in Amsterdam.

They would drop in on this city for a stopover. Though this was only one night stay, they were excited for the first step of this journey.

■ 本文の内容に合うものには○を、合わないものには×をつけなさい。
1．機内で、アツシはコジロウよりも先に寝てしまった。
2．アツシは音楽を聴きながら、眠りについた。
3．客室乗務員によるアナウンスで、着陸までの時間を知った。

● コラム【機内エンターテイメント】

　今では多くの航空会社が国際線のフライトで提供している娯楽である（格安航空会社では有料であることが多い）。昔は、数本ほどの映画が繰り返し自動的に流されているだけで、運が悪いと途中から見なくてはならないといった、客が受け身のものだった。しかし、近年は自由に好きな映画を最初からでも、途中からでも見ることができる。映画の本数も多く充実しており、大手航空会社などは、日本で公開される前の最新映画を提供していることもある。筆者も、後の Unit で出てくる映画『Paddington』を日本での封切り前に鑑賞できた。また、映画だけでなくゲームや音楽を楽しむこともできるので、長時間フライトの退屈を紛らわすのに、うってつけである。

Unit 4

■ Vocabulary Study: Scene 1

1. entry formalities （　）　a. 旅行途中の短い滞在
2. destination （　）　b. 観光
3. stopover （　）　c. 入国手続き
4. sightseeing （　）　d. 目的地

■ Vocabulary Study: Scene 2

1. fatigue （　）　a. バイキング式の食事
2. buffet （　）　b. 疲労

Scene 1: Entry Formalities at Stopover

　The Boeing 747 descended to the runway of Amsterdam Airport Schiphol. Atsushi and Kojiro looked out of the window. There were lots of red roofs. The scenery was indeed what they imagined of Holland. They gave a little shout of joy. The seatbelt sign was turned off and all passengers started to take out their baggage. Kojiro became a little bit nervous and said to himself, "Now, we have landed in a foreign country."

At the arrival gate, many of the passengers stood in a long line. Atsushi and Kojiro took out their passports and air tickets from their baggage. The tall male inspector was equipped with a hand gun and a nightstick.

■ **Dialogue**

Atsushi	"Good morning."
Inspector	"Good morning. Passport and air ticket, please."
Atsushi	"Here you are."
Inspector	"How long are you staying?"
Atsushi	"One night."
Inspector	"Stopover?"
Atsushi	"Yes."
Inspector	"What is your final destination?"
Atsushi	"Glasgow in Scotland."
Inspector	"What is the purpose of your visit to Glasgow?"
Atsushi	"Sightseeing."
Inspector	"OK. Have a nice trip!"
Atsushi	"Thank you."

■ 本文の内容に合うものには○を、合わないものには×をつけなさい。

1．コジロウにとっては初めての海外だったが、平静な様子だった。
2．アツシとコジロウの最終目的地は、オランダである。
3．アツシとコジロウの旅は、観光目的である。

Scene 2: Breakfast in Amsterdam

　Atsushi and Kojiro fell asleep at 7:00 p.m. the night before. They had a deep sleep and recovered from the fatigue of the long flight. That morning, they went to buy their breakfast at a store in a hotel. They needed to wear jackets in the cold morning. They were looking for sandwiches and some drinks. Kojiro said, "Hey, I calculated the cost of buying our breakfast. It is more expensive than having breakfast at the restaurant of this hotel." "Oh! That's true. Let's go to the restaurant instead!" "Yeah, I want to eat a hot meal." They went to the restaurant on the second floor.

　The restaurant provided a buffet style breakfast. The pleasant aroma of coffee stimulated their stomachs. There were only a few people at that time. The female staff said to them, "Pay later please." The two young men found a table at the end of the room, and then they went to fetch many kinds of things to eat. Atsushi's plate was full of food, such as pancakes, slices of cheese, scrambled egg, and sausage. On the other hand, Kojiro poured hot coffee into a cup, and picked up ham, beans and salad on his plate. His plate was also filled with delicious food.

　They felt relaxed at the table. They had plenty of time before going back to the airport. Drinking another cup of coffee, Kojiro checked today's plan. Atsushi drank a cup of green tea and looked at his small notebook to check their schedule. In the meantime, lots of guests came to the restaurant. Atsushi paid for breakfast with his credit card.

■ 本文の内容に合うものには○を、合わないものには×をつけなさい。
1．アツシとコジロウは、ホテルの売店で朝食を購入した。
2．レストランでは、すでに多くの人が朝食を食べていた。

3．アツシとコジロウは、朝食を好きなだけ食べることができた。
4．アツシはコーヒーをおかわりした。
5．アツシとコジロウは、朝食の支払いを現金で行った。

● コラム【空港隣接ホテルの事情】

　筆者がアムステルダムで宿泊したのは、空港からタクシーで10分ほどの場所にある、主にストップオーバーをする客に使用されるホテルだった。事前に予約した際に、ホテルの部屋にバスタブがあることをネットで確認していたが、実際に行ってみると、電話ボックスのようなシャワー室があるだけだった。バスタブ付きの部屋に替えてもらうように交渉したが、満室だったので結局その部屋に一泊することになった。日本と異なり、ヨーロッパでは部屋にバスタブが付いていないホテルも多いので、どうしてもバスタブを確保したい場合は、直接ホテルに連絡を取ってリクエストすることをお勧めしたい（アメリカ英語では bathtub だが、イギリス英語では bath という）。

Unit 5

■ Vocabulary Study: Scene 1

1. lively   (   )   a. 雲で覆われた
2. leisurely   (   )   b. ゆっくりと
3. overcast   (   )   c. 北海
4. the North Sea   (   )   d. 活気に満ちた

■ Vocabulary Study: Scene 2

1. old-fashioned   (   )   a. 浴槽
2. semi-basement   (   )   b. 古風な
3. bath   (   )   c. 耐え難い
4. unbearable   (   )   d. 交渉
5. negotiation   (   )   e. 半地下の

Scene 1: Flight to Glasgow

Atsushi and Kojiro left the Amsterdam airport hotel. They went to the stop for the shuttle bus to the airport.

At first there was nobody at the bus stop, but gradually several travellers came. The cold wind was blowing hard. Before long, a shuttle bus came. When the door opened, Kojiro quickly carried two suitcases up into the bus.

The airport was very lively. The security inspection and the departure formalities went smoothly. The boarding time was 30 minutes later. The flight time to Scotland was 1 hour and 30 minutes. The plane would fly across the North Sea. Atsushi said, "The flight time is short, like that of a domestic line, so we can't expect high quality in-flight entertainment." Kojiro followed his advice and got out a novel for this short flight. Before long, there was an announcement for boarding, and passengers started to pass through the boarding gate. There were no Japanese passengers apart from Atsushi and Kojiro.

There was an announcement from the captain, and flight 737 took off leisurely from Amsterdam. It was overcast, but the plane penetrated the clouds, and Atsushi and Kojiro could see the sun shining across the blue sky.

As for in-flight entertainment, there was only a European comedy program on the monitor up above. The comedy was not interesting for Atsushi and Kojiro. Also, Kojiro's novel involved a gloomy story, and it wasn't suitable for a happy flight. He gave up reading it and closed his eyes, while Atsushi was already fast asleep.

■ 本文の内容に合うものには○を、合わないものには×をつけなさい。
1．アツシとコジロウは、オランダ出発当日はタクシーを利用した。
2．機内には多くの日本人が乗っていた。
3．コジロウは機内で小説を堪能した。
4．アツシは機内で早々に寝てしまった。

Scene 2: Arrival at a Hotel in Glasgow

The temperature was 17℃ in Glasgow. In Glasgow airport, Atsushi wore a down jacket and Kojiro wore a leather rider's jacket. They felt cold, so they took a taxi to the hotel. The taxi arrived at the stone building along Elmbank Street. There were old-fashioned streets and stone buildings around the town. Kojiro carried two suitcases up the stone steps of the hotel entrance. Atsushi checked in at the front desk and received a room key. Their room was in a semi-basement floor of the stone building. Kojiro finally dropped the suitcases in the hallway of the semi-basement floor. Atsushi soon came back from the room. Kojiro asked him, "What happened?" Atsushi said, "There was no bath in that room! I should see about changing rooms. On the Internet, I booked a room with a bath." Atsushi dashed up the steps to the front desk. No bath in a bathroom was common in the UK. For them, however, that would be unbearable to spend a whole week without a bath. Kojiro really hoped that Atsushi's negotiation would succeed.

Miraculously there was just one room with a bath left. As a result of the negotiation, they could have the room with a bath. This room was also on the semi-basement floor. Atsushi did a great job and now they had no worries. Atsushi asked a hotel staff member where the nearest supermarket was. They went out to get some food for dinner.

■ 本文の内容に合うように、質問に答えなさい。
1．アツシとコジロウが泊まるホテルは、どのような建物か。

２．ホテルでのチェックインの後、アツシが最初に行ったことは何か。

　　_____

３．アツシとコジロウはホテルの部屋に入り、その後どのように行動したか。

　　_____

● コラム【入国審査の待ち時間】

　入国審査は、飛行機から降りて最初に行われる。当然空港には自分たちが乗ってきた飛行機だけでなく、次々と別の飛行機も到着するので、場合によっては、入国審査を受けるために、長蛇の列に並ぶこともある。幸い筆者は、グラスゴー空港では20分程度並ぶだけですんだ。グラスゴーはスコットランドにおける商業都市として位置づけられており、エディンバラほどは観光客が来ないからであろう。一大観光都市にあるエディンバラ空港なら20分ですまなかったかもしれない。場所は変わるが、筆者はイギリスの玄関口ともいえるロンドンのヒースロー空港で、夏の盛りに2時間半入国審査のために並んだ経験がある。

Unit 6

■ Vocabulary Study: Scene 1

1. hub station （　）　　a．パブ（イギリスの居酒屋）
2. budget   （　）　　b．七面鳥の肉
3. turkey   （　）　　c．予算
4. pub   （　）　　d．中心となる駅

■ Vocabulary Study: Scene 2

1. hypothetical （　）　　a．仮説の
2. long-awaited （　）　　b．執念
3. obsession   （　）　　c．久しく待ち望んだ

Scene 1: Preparation for Dinner

Atsushi and Kojiro got on a ScotRail train from Glasgow Queen Street station to Charing Cross station. Charing Cross station was a big hub station in Glasgow. Atsushi wanted to eat lunch, so they went to a pub called 'Dorothy's' near the station. Kojiro was not hungry, so he didn't order anything. Atsushi ordered a jacket potato with haggis and a glass of orange juice. Atsushi and Kojiro were surprised at the jacket potato, because it was so big.

When Atsushi had eaten all of it, they felt like going to a supermarket to get some food for dinner. They found Sainsbury's, which was one of the most long-established supermarkets. Atsushi chose Greek salad, couscous salad, slices of turkey, a rice pudding and so on.

It cost 30 pounds, which was about 5,000 yen, for food for that night and next morning. That would save a great deal of their budget. If you ate dinner at a restaurant, you would be charged 30 pounds per person for dinner.

The two young men started preparing for dinner as soon as they got back to the hotel. They would do anything but eat a cold meal. Atsushi took out a portable hot plate from his suitcase.

【Notes】haggis: ハギス（刻んだ羊の臓物やオートムギを羊の胃袋に入れて煮込んだスコットランド料理）

■ 本文の内容に合うものには○を、合わないものには×をつけなさい。

1．アツシは、パブで昼食を食べた。
2．アツシとコジロウは、レストランで朝食を食べることに決めた。
3．アツシは、グラスゴーまでホットプレートを持ってきた。

Scene 2: First Dinner in Glasgow

It began to get dark and Atsushi and Kojiro felt the temperature dropping. After Atsushi had a bath, he leaned his head to one side and said, "It's so cold in this country. Can Scottish people bear not to have a bath?" Kojiro replied, "I think so. Also, the air in this country is much drier than Japan, so I think maybe they hardly sweat." "I see." With this hypothetical opinion, they cheerfully put pieces of turkey ham on the hot plate. They started their long-awaited first dinner in Glasgow.

At first, the piece of bread was hard, but it became soft on the hot plate. Atsushi picked up the hot bread, and put a slice of ham on it. Then, he put grain mustard on it. Atsushi tasted the hot mustard and said, "This is delicious!" Kojiro also ate the hot one and said, "It's great! This mustard has a different taste from Japanese mustard." Kojiro also noticed that the flavour of the dressing on the Greek salad was stronger than a Japanese dressing, and he realised he liked this strong flavour. Atsushi warmed a piece of bread, and then he melted some cheese a little. Next, the combination of the warm bread and melted cheese with mustard was eaten by his big mouth. He made this golden combination again and again. Kojiro, on the other hand, was thinking of the early times of great navigation. In those days, the Europeans went all the way to distant continents to get spices. Kojiro was convinced of their obsession for spices. He thought that if he had been of that time, he would have applied himself to the adventure of seeking spices. Kojiro gave a bitter smile and the night in Glasgow was far advanced.

【Notes】the great navigation times: 大航海時代

■ 本文の内容に合うように、質問に答えなさい。

1．アツシとコジロウは、部屋に戻った後、まず何をしたか。

　　_____

2．コジロウは、夕食で何に気付いたか。

　　_____

3．コジロウは、マスタードを味わって何を思い浮かべたか。

　　_____

● コラム【便利なホットプレート】

　本編に夕食をホットプレートで温めるくだりが出てくるが、外国では日本とコンセントの形状や電圧が異なるので、変圧器と変換プラグも必要となる。その辺りの事情は本編では省略したが、準備はなかなか大変である。そもそもホットプレートの発想はどこからきたのか。実は、筆者が真冬にドイツのフライブルクに滞在したときの体験がもとになっている。名物のクリスマス・マーケットでアツアツのヴルスト（ソーセージのこと）を買ってホテルの部屋に戻ってきたら、すっかり冷え切っていて、とても残念であった。では、外食をすればよいかというと、予算がかかるから頻繁には行けないし、海外の夜は防犯という点で気が抜けない。そこで、部屋でディナーというプランに落ち着いた。スーパーで地元の人たちが食べる食材や惣菜を買い、それらをホットプレートで温めて食べる食事は最高である。ただ、部屋に食べ物の匂いがつくという理由から、部屋での食事を禁止しているホテルもあるので、あらかじめホテル側に問い合わせてから使用してもらいたい。

Unit 7

■ Vocabulary Study: Scene 1

1. limited express　　（　）　　a．長方形の
2. dignified　　　　　（　）　　b．特急列車
3. rectangular　　　　（　）　　c．威厳のある
4. fortress　　　　　 （　）　　d．勇ましい
5. craggy　　　　　　 （　）　　e．要塞
6. brave　　　　　　　（　）　　f．(教会などの) 尖塔
7. steeple　　　　　　（　）　　g．岩の多い

■ Vocabulary Study: Scene 2

1. monument　　　　　　（　）　　a．世界遺産
2. Gothic architecture （　）　　b．記念碑
3. world heritage　　　（　）　　c．ゴシック建築

Scene 1: Let's go to Edinburgh!

Atsushi and Kojiro had a warm breakfast in their hotel room, and they left for Glasgow Queen Street station at 9:00 a.m. There were many trains at the platforms of the hub station. The station had the atmosphere of the movies, such as 'Harry Potter' and 'Paddington.' The limited express would take the two young men to the city of Edinburgh. It was a 50-minute journey to their destination, Waverley station.

Before long the conductor of the limited express announced their arrival in Edinburgh. Looking out from a window, Atsushi noticed the dignified castle which was a rectangular fortress on a craggy mountain. Atsushi took the plunge and asked a woman who was sitting on the opposite side. "Is that Edinburgh castle?" She replied "Yes. That's absolutely Edinburgh castle. Is this your first visit to Edinburgh?" When Atsushi said "yes", she said a phrase which was probably "Welcome to Edinburgh!" in Gaelic. Though they didn't figure out exactly what she said, they could imagine that's what it was by her facial expression. Their hearts began to leap to see the noted city of Edinburgh.

When they went out from Waverley station, they could see clear blue sky and the old-fashioned streets. Edinburgh Castle on the craggy mountain seemed to encourage them to visit the castle. There was a large Ferris wheel near Princes Street Gardens. Kojiro agreed to Atsushi's idea to go on the Ferris wheel to enjoy a view of the whole city.

Soon after they were in line, they were able to get on the Ferris wheel. They were surprised to see that the Ferris wheel had only iron rails. When they went up in the sky, the cold wind blew without mercy. "That's the sea, isn't it?" Atsushi spotted the sea in the distance and they understood that the cold wind was actually the sea breeze. They had never dreamed of seeing the sea in Scotland. They found a large old church which had a steeple. Furthermore, they could enjoy looking at the brave Edinburgh castle in detail. So, they could confirm the route to the castle. The two young men were satisfied with going on the Ferris wheel.

【Notes】Gaelic: ゲール語（スコットランドの古語）, Ferris wheel: 観覧車

■ 本文の内容に合うものには○を、合わないものには×をつけなさい。
1．アツシとコジロウは、まず映画の『ハリー・ポッター』を観た。
2．列車の車窓からエディンバラ城が見えた。
3．同じ列車に乗り合わせた婦人が、英語で歓迎の気持ちを伝えてくれたとアツシとコジロウは受け取った。
4．アツシとコジロウは、なかなか観覧車に乗れなかった。
5．アツシとコジロウは、観覧車から街並みを良く観察できた。

Scene 2: Tourist City, Edinburgh

　Edinburgh is a tourist city in Scotland, and is one of the most famous sightseeing spots in the world. Atsushi and Kojiro decided to visit The National Gallery of Scotland first, which they could see from the Ferris wheel.

　Just before they stepped off the Ferris wheel, they located the Scott Monument with its large Gothic architecture in the distance. This monument was built to commemorate a great Scottish writer, Sir Walter Scott. It seemed far from where they were, so they gave up approaching the monument. The beautiful city, Edinburgh has a new town, and also an old town which was designated as a world heritage site by UNESCO. This means that walking in the city is not easy for tourists.

　Atsushi slowly took out his pedometer from his pocket and was surprised at the number. "It is still before noon, but my pedometer already recorded more than 5,000 steps!" Kojiro said, "OK! Hurry up! We had better not run out of time in the middle of the city." The two young men hurried to The National Gallery of Scotland.

【Notes】UNESCO: 国連教育科学文化機関・ユネスコ

■ 本文の内容に合うように、質問に答えなさい。

1．アツシとコジロウは、観覧車から降りた後、まずどこへ向かうことにしたか。

　　_____

2．アツシとコジロウは、何をあきらめたか。

　　_____

● コラム【ヨーロッパの香辛料】

　筆者が海外へ行くと必ず購入するのが、マスタードなどの香辛料である。Unit 6でも2人が驚愕の声を上げているが、確かにヨーロッパのマスタードは濃厚で美味しく、風味が異なる。一口にマスタードといっても様々な種類があり、からしの粒が大きなものやパプリカ風味といったフレーバーつきのものもある。お土産として購入するのもお勧めである。普通の土産物屋には売っていないが、地元の人たちが利用するスーパーマーケットに行けば手に入る。

Unit 8

■ Vocabulary Study: Scene 1

1. Grecian shrine style ( )　　a．物売りの屋台
2. vendor's stall ( )　　b．巡回展
3. exhibition tour ( )　　c．ギリシャの神殿様式
4. transformation ( )　　d．変化、変形

■ Vocabulary Study: Scene 2

1. robber ( )　　a．手の込んだ
2. execute ( )　　b．強盗
3. porcelain ( )　　c．広場
4. elaborate ( )　　d．磁器
5. public square ( )　　e．処刑する

Scene 1: National Gallery of Scotland

Next to The Royal Scottish Academy which was Grecian shrine style, there were many street vendor's stalls on the stone pavement. Atsushi and Kojiro passed this lively space, and they looked up at National Gallery of Scotland. This museum was also Grecian style architecture and had on a pole the flag of the St. Andrew's Cross of Scotland. The flag whose colours were blue and white was fluttering in the wind which seemed to show the pride of the Scottish people. The Union Jack, the national flag was also fluttering in the wind on the other pole of the gallery.

The gallery was not crowded at all. The pictures were hung on the red coloured walls and the floor carpets were light green. The great masters' paintings, such as Raphael, Rembrandt and Gauguin were crowded on the walls. "Great! These are just what one would expect of the treasures." "Yes, indeed! With whichever painting, we could hold an exhibition tour in Japan." There were many great paintings in this gallery. Atsushi and Kojiro had a wonderful time enjoying these works of art. Atsushi found that there was a painting of the old Edinburgh Castle. It was painted by an artist who they did not know. In that painting, the grave Edinburgh castle was on the Castle Rock. The whole construction was different from the present castle. It was attacked and destroyed by the enemy again and again. Therefore, the castle experienced its transformation many times as a result of unavoidable circumstances. The two young men did not notice its transformation and went to look at the other paintings.

【Notes】National Gallery of Scotland: 国立スコットランド美術館, St. Andrew's Cross: スコットランドの旗, the Union Jack: 英国国旗

■ 本文の内容に合うものには○を、合わないものには×をつけなさい。

1. アツシとコジロウは、まずロイヤル・スコティッシュ・アカデミーに入

館した。
2．国立スコットランド美術館の上に、英国国旗が翻っていた。
3．国立スコットランド美術館には、ゴッホの作品があった。
4．国立スコットランド美術館には、昔のエディンバラ城を描いた絵画も展示されていた。
5．アツシとコジロウは、昔のエディンバラ城が、現在と外観が異なることに気づいた。

Scene 2: Lunch at a Pub

Atsushi and Kojiro went out from National Gallery of Scotland and they determined to take an early lunch at a pub along the Royal Mile. Atsushi found a pub whose name was 'Deacon Brodie's Tavern.' 'Tavern' means pub in English and 'Deacon Brodie' was a person who lived in the eighteenth century. He was a leader of robbers who was executed in 1788. There was an explanation board on the stone wall outside the pub. The two young men didn't notice the explanation board and they entered the pub. They ordered plates of haggis and mashed potato. Besides, Atsushi chose a pot of hot tea and Kojiro chose a cup of hot milk coffee. They were seated in front of the dark brown wooden table by the window. It was not long before plates of hot haggis and a cup of hot milkly coffee were brought to the table. Then, hot boiled water in a white porcelain pot, an empty cup, and a tea bag of Scottish breakfast tea were carried to the table. It seemed that tea was to be made by the guest. So, Atsushi happily poured the hot water into the cup and made the tea. Kojiro felt the warmth of the hot coffee sinking deep into his body. There was a small jar of barbecue sauce on the plate with the haggis, and this sauce went well with it. They ate up what was on their plates and looked over at another table. A Scottish man was eating a beefsteak with a pint of Guinness beer. It was not usual for Atsushi and Kojiro to see this scene in Japan at lunch time, so they were surprised at it.

 They left the pub, and walked along the Royal Mile. People were gathering at a public square. They were interested in the excitement and found a street performer among a crowd. It was not a human character but 'the Predator' from Hollywood movies. The street performer wore an elaborate predator costume. Many tourists took photos together with it by turns. The two young men found it very interesting, and took a picture of the scene, then quietly left.

【Notes】Royal Mile: ロイヤル・マイル（エディンバラ城からホリルードハウス宮殿まで続く1マイルの目抜き通り）, Guinness beer: ギネスビール , predator: 捕食動物

■ 本文の内容に合うように、質問に答えなさい。

1．アツシとコジロウが入ったパブの名前の由来は何か。

_____

2．アツシとコジロウが注文したドリンクは、それぞれ何か。

_____

3．他のテーブルで客が飲んでいた飲み物は何か。

_____

4．ロイヤル・マイルにはどのようなパフォーマーがいたか。

　　_____

● コラム【日帰り旅行ではもったいない！】

　筆者もグラスゴーからエディンバラへの日帰り旅行をしたが、国立スコットランド美術館を出たところで力尽き、山の上にそびえたつエディンバラ城を目前にして、いったんグラスゴーまで帰らざるをえなかった。天然の要塞として名高いエディンバラ城の岩山（キャッスル・ロック）は、歩いて登るには相当きつい勾配を有している。本編ではエディンバラの主要観光地をすべて1日で辿ったように書かれているが、実際には相当ハードなスケジュールとなってしまうので、少なくとも3〜4日は、エディンバラに滞在して巡りたいものである。

Unit 9

■ Vocabulary Study: Scene 1

1. tattoo （ ） a．共同墓地
2. fortress （ ） b．軍楽行進
3. coat of arms （ ） c．要塞
4. cemetery （ ） d．紋章

■ Vocabulary Study: Scene 2

1. barrack （ ） a．心を奪う
2. troops （ ） b．兵舎
3. royal family （ ） c．後世
4. captivate （ ） d．屈辱を与える
5. humiliate （ ） e．王室、王族
6. posterity （ ） f．軍隊

Scene 1: Edinburgh Castle

After getting energy by eating lunch, Atsushi and Kojiro climbed the steep Royal Mile rapidly. On the way, they sometimes took a rest at a slope. The two young men cast side glances at the Scotch Whisky Experience, and went toward Edinburgh Castle. Just before the castle, they arrived at the site of the Edinburgh Military Tattoo. The rectangular site was formed like a stadium where the tattoo is held every August. It's a big event in Edinburgh city. Bagpipe bands and music bands from all parts of the world demonstrated at the music festival. The festival always began in the evening, so Atsushi and Kojiro couldn't see it. The two young men crossed the rectangular festival site which was about two hundred metres long. At the end of the site, a World War II combat propeller plane was on display. They stopped to look up at the front of the stone gate of Edinburgh Castle. The Scottish coat of arms was on the stone gate, and the Scottish flag of the St. Andrew's Cross was fluttering in the blue sky. The Union Jack of UK might have been fluttering next to the St. Andrew's Cross, but they couldn't confirm the flag's pattern.

Atsushi and Kojiro went through the heavy stone gate, and they stood in a queue to buy tickets at the ticket counter. They bought tickets easily and entered the fortress castle. The two young men were convinced that this castle had been constructed as a fortress. The crenelated walls had guns to shoot in all directions. There was the soldiers' dog cemetery which can be seen but not accessed from above. Pretty flowers were offered at the tombstones in the cemetery.

【Notes】World War II: 第二次世界大戦, bagpipe: バグパイプ（スコットランドの楽器）, crenelated wall: 銃眼のある壁

■ 本文の内容に合うものには○を、合わないものには×をつけなさい。
1. アツシとコジロウは、まずスコッチウィスキー・エクスペリエンスに入った。
2. アツシとコジロウは、エディンバラ・ミリタリー・タトゥーのパフォーマンスを観た。
3. エディンバラ城の門の前に、古い戦闘機が展示されていた。
4. エディンバラ城は、要塞には見えない外観だった。
5. エディンバラ城の中に、軍用犬の墓地があった。

Scene 2: Inside the Fortress (1)

　Atsushi and Kojiro visited St. Margaret's Chapel which was the oldest structure of this castle. This chapel was constructed at the beginning of the twelfth century, and it had a Norman arched narrow hall.
　Next, they visited the Great Hall. The hall was established as the place of formal ceremony by James IV (1488-1513). In 1650, Oliver Cromwell (1599-1658) from England occupied Scotland and, by force, changed this hall into the barracks of the English troops. The hall became a deathly place between Scotland and England. In 1887, the Great Hall was reconstructed as a place of the formal ceremony again. Since the reconstruction, the Great Hall has functioned as the ceremony hall for the royal family of the United Kingdom. The two young men entered the Great Hall and they were captivated by the red-coloured walls. They were surprised at various swords, lances, suits of armour and helmets tightly hung on the walls. Kojiro was surprised and said, "Why are there lots of arms and suits of armour in this hall?" It was quite natural for Kojiro to have this question, because it was a ceremonial place. This hall was no longer the barracks of the troops. Kojiro

gasped at this scene and felt a sense of incongruity about it. On the other hand, Atsushi was reading the explanation board of the Great Hall and said, "This hall's display seems to show the history of humiliated Scotland." "What's history?" "Originally, the Great Hall was the holy place of the royal family of Scotland, but troops from England invaded and they looked down on this holy place as a barrack of troops." "Hmm……" "That is why the Scottish retained the situation of the barracks to show the history to posterity." "I see." Kojiro nodded in response to Atsushi's explanation.

【Notes】Norman: ノルマン様式の , lance: 槍 , sense of incongruity: 違和感

■ 本文の内容に合うものには○を、合わないものには×をつけなさい。

１．武器は、グレート・ホールから撤去されていた。

２．アツシとコジロウは、城の最古の建造物には入らなかった。

３．アツシは、ホール内の様子を自分なりに解釈した。

４．グレート・ホールは、最初儀式の場として建てられた。

● コラム【ミリタリー・タトゥーとは？】

　タトゥーというと、連想するのは入れ墨かもしれない。確かに英語のスペルは同じなのだが、それとは別に「軍楽行進」という意味があり、主に余興として夜間に野外で行われるものを示す。エディンバラの夏の祭典の中でも特に有名なフェスティバルが、「エディンバラ・ミリタリー・タトゥー」であり、8月の3週間、エディンバラ城前の広場で行われる。本編のはじめの写真に観客席が写っているので、見返してもらいたい。人気が高いので、チケットは半年前から予約しないと手に入らないそうである。

Unit 10

■ Vocabulary Study: Scene 1

1. chamber   (　)   a. 暖炉
2. fireplace   (　)   b. 肖像画
3. portrait   (　)   c. 部屋

■ Vocabulary Study: Scene 2

1. distillation (　)   a. 手順
2. vehicle   (　)   b. 乗物
3. barrel   (　)   c. 樽
4. medieval   (　)   d. 蒸溜
5. procedure   (　)   e. 中世の

Scene 1: Inside the Fortress (2)

Atsushi and Kojiro visited Queen Mary's chamber in the Royal Palace. The Queen of Scotland, Mary Stuart (1542-1587) gave birth to her son in this room. He became the King of Scotland, James VI (1566-1625). The portrait of Queen Mary was hung on the wall. The arms of the royal family were displayed above the large fireplace. The three sacred treasures of Scotland (the crown, the sword, and the sceptre) were kept in the crown room. Atsushi and Kojiro saw the Stone of Scone that had been sat upon by the King of Scotland from ancient times. The stone had been used as the imperial seat at the enthronement in Scotland. Once, this stone was carried away to the Westminster Abbey in London, England. In 1996, however, the stone was returned to Scotland. The Stone of Scone whose shape was a small table was also kept in the crown room. Of course, they were not allowed to take photos of these great treasures. The two young men thought of the history of the struggle between Scotland and England.

After visiting the Royal Palace, they went out again. They slowly went down the spiral stone path, and found the crenelated walls provided the guns against the outside of the castle. By the side of the guns, they noticed the big rectangular rock whose thickness was greater than Atsushi's height. Atsushi found the explanation plate, and knew that the rock's name was the Half-Moon Battery. Under the battery was the tomb of King David II (1329-1371).

Finally, the two young men visited the war memorial hall. There were many lists of soldiers who died in World Wars I and II. The lists were the large registers. Kojiro could also confirm the names of the soldiers from the Gulf War in 1991.

【Notes】sceptre: 王笏(おうしゃく), Westminster Abbey: ウェストミンスター寺院 , battery: 砲台 , the Gulf War: 湾岸戦争 , the Stone of Scone: 運命の石

■ アツシとコジロウについて、本文の内容に合うものには○を、合わないものには×をつけなさい。

1．メアリー女王の部屋には入らなかった。
2．メアリー女王の部屋で三種の宝器を見た。
3．クラウン・ルームで運命の石を見た。
4．大きな砲台を見つけた。
5．戦没者を記念するホールに入った。

Scene 2: The Scotch Whisky Experience (1)

Atsushi and Kojiro left from the stone gate of Edinburgh Castle. They passed through the site of the Edinburgh Military Tattoo, and reached the street of The Royal Mile. At once two young men noticed an old building built of brick. That was the Scotch Whisky Experience. This was a famous tourist spot in Edinburgh, and they could learn the procedure of distillation and the long history of Scotch whisky. In this experience-style museum, they also had the opportunity of tasting Scotch whisky.

This museum had a direct sales store of Scotch whisky. The two young men saw the rich selection of Scotch whisky on the ground floor and the first floor. They bought their tickets and went into the entrance of the attraction. Their hearts beat with delight when they rode on the vehicle whose shape was a whisky barrel. This vehicle took them to scenes one after another, and they could learn how to make Scotch whisky. Atsushi cried out with glee, "This is just like the Haunted House of an amusement park!"

The vehicle carried them into a dark tunnel, and classical music sounded from the dark. In front of their vehicle appeared a medieval Scottish man in holographic form. This tour guide started to explain the procedure of distillation. The history of Scotch whisky very much appealed to them. The vehicle moved forward and the virtual tour guide changed form. The two young men were really satisfied with the Scotch whisky tour attraction. The end of the dark tunnel was the museum's other entrance.

【Notes】Haunted House: お化け屋敷

■ アツシとコジロウがスコッチウィスキー・エクスペリエンスで体験したことについて、質問に答えなさい。

1．建物の中で、最初に見ていたのは何か。

　_____

2．何に対して喜んだか。

　_____

● コラム【スコッチウィスキーとは？】

　ウィスキーという言葉は、ゲール語のウィスケ・バーハ（命の水）からきており、修道士がアイルランドからスコットランドに伝えたといわれている。大麦を蒸溜して作ったものがスコッチウィスキーである。ちなみに、アメリカのバーボンウィスキーはトウモロコシを原料に、またカナディアンウィスキーはライ麦を原料に蒸溜されたものである。以前に朝の連続ドラマで取り上げられたおかげで、スコッチウィスキーの認知度は、日本でもかなり上がったようである。

Unit 11

■ Vocabulary Study: Scene 1

1. stylish ( )   a. 味覚
2. bearded ( )   b. スマートな
3. copper ( )   c. 銅
4. amber ( )   d. ひげのある
5. palate ( )   e. 琥珀

■ Vocabulary Study: Scene 2

1. glitter ( )   a. 空砲（実弾の装填なし）
2. chic ( )   b. きらきら輝く
3. blank cartridge ( )   c. 粋な

Scene 1: The Scotch Whisky Experience (2)

After the attraction, Atsushi and Kojiro were guided to a stylish hall. The hall was lit with soft orange light. It was a square room and the long tables were set up by the side of the walls. About fifteen guests were seated at the chairs beside the tables, and Atsushi and Kojiro joined them. After all the guests were seated, a slim bearded face guide in the uniform of a bartender appeared to the centre of the hall. His position was good and he was seen by all the guests. He started to explain how to enjoy Scotch whisky.

The guide explained that there were five steps to appreciating Scotch whisky.

1. Colour: Is your whisky light gold, bright copper or rich amber in colour?
2. Body: Does your whisky have a light, medium or full body?
3. Nose: Which aromas do you recognise when you nose your whisky—is it malty, smoky, fruity, chocolatey?
4. Palate: What characteristics do you notice on the palate—is it softly sweet, rich and fruity, or peppery & spicy?
5. Finish: Does the flavour remain for a long time or does it disappear quickly?

The guide distributed to the guests a card like a postcard. On the card, were the words, "SLÀINTE MHATH!" This means "Cheers!", a drinking toast in Gaelic. Atsushi turned the card over, and he read the words at the centre, 'A SENSATIONAL JOURNEY.' At the upper left of the card was the logo of LOWLAND in the green box. In the yellow box at the upper right was the logo of HIGHLAND. At the lower left, was the logo of SPEYSIDE in the light blue box. The lower right of the card had the logo of ISLAY in the red box.

Atsushi got interested in the colourful card, and noticed a trick on it. It said, 'Touch to reveal scent.' Immediately, he rubbed the logo of SPEYSIDE. He smelled it and said, "The aroma of a banana!" "That's right!" The guide pointed his finger at Atsushi and praised his correct answer. The guide started to explain the characteristics of each box. The Speyside whisky had a fruity aroma. The Islay whisky featured a smoky aroma. The Highland gave off a sweet and fruity aroma. Kojiro was impressed by the Lowland aroma, which was like the grassy plain. Finally, the guide introduced the features of distilleries in the four main regions in Scotland.

After the explanation, the guide poured Scotch whisky into the glasses in front of the guests. Atsushi requested Speyside whisky which had the aroma of banana, and Kojiro enjoyed the smoky aroma of Islay whisky. The glass was given to the guest as a present. The package of the glass showed that this was 'Glencairn Glass.'

After they returned to Japan, Atsushi found out that this glass maker was famous for the whisky glass. Of course, they kept this glass as a memento of the trip.

【Notes】www.scotchwhiskyexperience.co.uk 参照 , memento: 記念品

■ 本文の内容と一致しているものを1つ選びなさい。

1. （a）客はアツシとコジロウだけだった。
   （b）アトラクション終了後、アツシとコジロウはホールへ入って行った。
   （c）アトラクション終了後、アツシとコジロウはスコッチウィスキー・エクスペリエンスの外へ出た。

2. （a）ガイドはゲール語で説明を開始した。
   （b）ポストカードのようなものが配られた。
   （c）スコッチウィスキーの評価法は4項目あった。

3. （a）「ハイランド」はバナナの香りがした。
   （b）「スペイサイド」は草原の香りがした。
   （c）「アイラ」はスモーキーな香りがした。

4．（a）試飲が終わるとグラスを返した。
　　（b）アツシは「スペイサイド」の試飲を楽しんだ。
　　（c）コジロウは「スペイサイド」の試飲を楽しんだ。

Scene 2: Take a Rest at a Cafe

Atsushi and Kojiro went out from the hall and were surprised. The sides of the corridor were glass showcases. There were many kinds of Scotch whisky bottles. Hundreds of whisky bottles glittered under soft lighting effects. The brilliancy of these whisky bottles was one of the highlights of the series of experiences. The guests passed through the corridor, and they found a chic bar. The two young men just looked at the bar, and left that part. Then they realised that they came to the first floor of the direct sales store. Many tourists were purchasing bottles of Scotch whisky.

Atsushi and Kojiro left the store and entered the nearest cafe. They decided to take a rest. They felt chilly, so they wanted to have a hot drink. They ordered a pot of chamomile tea, which was Atsushi's idea. While they were waiting, they were talking about what to do in Edinburgh afterwards. They no longer had time to visit any other tourist spots. Especially they wanted to get some food for dinner. There was a department store MARKS & SPENCER on Princes Street, opposite the large Ferris wheel. Kojiro found the food market in M&S that morning. Kojiro agreed with Atsushi to buy some food there before going back to Glasgow.

The two young men were warmed by hot chamomile tea, and left the cafe. They went down the steep stone steps. Suddenly, a thundering sound roared in the distance. Kojiro noticed the sound and checked the time by looking at his watch. He called Atsushi to stop, "It's the One O'clock Gun!"

"Really?" "Yeah, because it is one o'clock now." Actually, Edinburgh castle goes off every day at 1:00 p.m. but of course a blank cartridge was used. This 'One O'clock Gun' was popular with tourists. Atsushi and Kojiro were lucky to hear it.

The two young men entered MARKS & SPENCER with light steps. They selected a fillet of sea bass and a lamb leg steak. Atsushi didn't miss some pieces of scone and mix beans salad. The pleasant dinner seemed to be waiting for them. Just then, the limited Scotrail express train bound for Glasgow arrived at the platform of Waverley station. They carried some of their food in their arms and, hurrying, they caught the limited express.

■ 本文の内容と一致しているものを1つ選びなさい。

1. （a）試飲室を出ると、すぐにバーがあった。
   （b）試飲室を出ると、すぐに直販所があった。
   （c）バーを通り過ぎると、そこは直販所の2階だった。

2. （a）アツシとコジロウは、カフェで体を温めた。
   （b）アツシとコジロウは、カフェで昼食を食べた。
   （c）アツシとコジロウは、エクスペリエンスを出ると、すぐに帰路についた。

3. （a）エディンバラ城へ向けて砲撃が行われた。
   （b）アツシとコジロウは、砲撃の音を聞くことができた。
   （c）アツシとコジロウは、夕食の食材をグラスゴーで購入することにした。

4. （a）アツシとコジロウは、ラム肉を購入した。

（b）アツシとコジロウは、エディンバラで夕食をとった。
（c）アツシとコジロウが入ったスーパーマーケットでは、シーバスは売り切れていた。

● コラム【便利なフードマーケット】

　海外で外食することは確かに旅の醍醐味ではあるが、1日3食外食にすると費用は驚くほどかかってしまうだろう。また、レストランでコース料理を注文すれば、興味のないメニューが出てくることもある。そこで、ホテルの部屋で食事をするというアイデアが生まれた。そうすれば1食分の費用を3分の1程度に抑えることも可能になる。そのときに食べたいものを必要な分だけ買えば無駄も出ない。イギリスでは、TESCOやSainsbury'sという名前のスーパーマーケットをよく見かけるが、そこでは肉や魚、ハム、ソーセージ、チーズも充実しており、惣菜やサラダのパックも手頃なものが手に入る。スイーツやパンも品揃えがよいので、機会を見つけて訪ねてみてほしい。

Unit 12

■ Vocabulary Study: Scene 1

1. Lordship   (   )   a. 邸宅
2. manor house   (   )   b. 領主
3. heritage   (   )   c. ザクロ
4. pomegranate   (   )   d. 文化的遺産

■ Vocabulary Study: Scene 2

1. double-decker   (   )   a. キリン
2. Victorian style   (   )   b. ダチョウ
3. stuffed specimen   (   )   c. ２階建てバス
4. giraffe   (   )   d. ヴィクトリア朝様式の
5. ostrich   (   )   e. はく製標本

Scene 1: Provand's Lordship

Atsushi and Kojiro visited the house of Provand's Lordship which was the oldest manor house in Glasgow. This three-story house was constructed in 1471. It was considered to be a precious heritage, and this gave us the information about the house in the 15th century. Atsushi and Kojiro read the description of Queen Mary of Scotland and the Provand's Lordship. Although Queen Mary and Provand's Lordship seemed to have a friendship, in recent years this was treated as a groundless rumour.

After Atsushi and Kojiro saw the inside of the house, they went out to the garden. The various kinds of flowers were in magnificent bloom. The pomegranate tree was bearing fruit. The two young men walked through the garden for a while.

Atsushi and Kojiro went back into town, and went to the cafe, 'Patisserie Valerie' to have lunch. Atsushi ordered the Greek cheese tart and the cranberry juice, and Kojiro ordered the same. The Greek cheese tart was not a round sweet pie, but a thick cheese slab on a slice of bread. After lunch, Kojiro wanted to drink a cup of coffee, so he placed an additional order for this.

■ アツシとコジロウについて、本文の内容に合うものには○を、合わないものには×をつけなさい。

1．グラスゴー最古の邸宅には入れなかった。
2．メアリー女王とプロバンド領主の交流についての説明文を見つけた。
3．カフェでは最初、同じ飲み物を頼んだ。

Unit 12

Scene 2: Kelvingrove Art Gallery & Museum

Atsushi and Kojiro rode on a City Sightseeing Glasgow bus. This sightseeing bus was a red two-story bus like a London double-decker. Behind the front three seats of the upper floor, there was no top to the bus. Atsushi and Kojiro first took their seats on the upper floor, and took turns taking photos. After taking photos, they quickly moved down to the lower floor. They could not stand the cold wind. However, some old people were still seated on the upper floor and enjoyed looking at the scenery.

The bus arrived at Kelvingrove Art Gallery & Museum and they got off the bus. They were faced with solemn brick architecture. This museum was a Victorian style structure built in 1902. The arts from the ancient Egyptians to the great masters such as Vincent Van Gogh were exhibited there. Among all these, the Christ of St John of the Cross by Salvador Dali (1904-1989) was the biggest highlight. In 1951, Glasgow city purchased that painting from Dali himself.

On the first floor, the two young men were surprised at the combat plane, Spitfire that had played an active role in World War II. This Spitfire was hung from the ceiling of the main exhibition hall. Under the combat plane, the stuffed specimens of an African elephant and a giraffe were displayed. Atsushi and Kojiro found the specimens of an ostrich and the biggest crab in the same place. "What is the criterion for choosing the exhibits?" The two young men could not find the answer. "Let's go to the ground floor!" They stepped down to the mysterious ground floor.

■ 本文の内容に合うように、質問に答えなさい。
1．アツシとコジロウは、バスでどのあたりの席に座ったか。

2．ケルヴィングローヴ美術館＆博物館では、どのような展示品を鑑賞で
きるか。

● コラム【ケルヴィングローヴ美術館＆博物館のインフォメーション】

　このミュージアムには、イギリス絵画をはじめ、様々な時代や場所の美術品が展示されている。ロンドンを除くと、イギリスにおいて来場者数が最大規模のミュージアムといわれている（ちなみにロンドンでは大英博物館をはじめ、あらゆる種類のミュージアムが点在している）。イギリスのミュージアムは無料で見学できるところが多いが、このミュージアムも無料であるため、入口が２カ所ある。Unit 14において、アツシとコジロウが正面の入口を帰りがけに見つけて驚くシーンが登場するが、彼らは知らずに裏の入口から入館していたということになる。ケルヴィングローヴ美術館＆博物館は、基本的に年中無休で、開館時間は午前10時あるいは11時から、午後5時までである。グラスゴーを訪れたら、是非この美の殿堂を訪れてほしい。

Unit 13

■ Vocabulary Study: Scene 1

1. bill　　　　　　　　　　（　）　　a. ミイラを収めた棺
2. skeleton　　　　　　　　（　）　　b. 生き物のはく製
3. stuffed creature　　　　　（　）　　c. シーラカンス
4. spectacle　　　　　　　　（　）　　d. くちばし
5. coelacanth　　　　　　　（　）　　e. 光景
6. mummy's coffin　　　　　（　）　　f. 骨格

■ Vocabulary Study: Scene 2

1. founder　　　　　　　　　　（　）　　a. 崇高な
2. sublime　　　　　　　　　　（　）　　b. 創設者
3. Pre-Raphaelite Brotherhood　（　）　　c. フクロウ
4. owl　　　　　　　　　　　　（　）　　d. ラファエロ前派

Scene 1: Stuffed Creatures

　Atsushi and Kojiro were speechless at the exhibition hall on the ground floor. There were various kinds of stuffed creatures, such as a caribou, a puma, a large sea turtle and a unique New Zealand bird, the kiwi. A cheetah and a kangaroo were also there. Near a penguin, was a stuffed bird with a red bill. The bird was a Pukeko, and it stood in a walking pose. Atsushi and Kojiro were overwhelmed by the large skeleton of a Ceratosaurus. Kojiro stared at them all in surprise and said, "There are so many stuffed creatures! The British people seem to have a liking for making stuffed specimens of precious creatures." Atsushi was also astonished at this spectacle.

　Two young men passed by a specimen of a coelacanth, and entered into the gallery of ancient Egyptian civilization. They observed the masks of the royal family and the mummys' coffins. There was a large tree stump which was 2 metres wide. The tree would be over one thousand years old. Suddenly, a statue appeared in front of them. It was Elvis Presley wearing a blue costume and holding a microphone. Next, they found the skin of a large snake whose name was 'the guardian of the river'. Its total length was 4 metres. They next found the armour of the old Scottish cavalry soldiers. In the Chinese section, a noble dress suit of the Chinese emperor was exhibited. Beside it, a Japanese suit of armour and a samurai helmet were displayed. There was an old samurai sword on the sword shelf, but it seemed not to have been well looked after. The samurai sword needed time and energy to keep it in good condition. The two young men looked at various exhibitions, and then visited the art gallery section.

【Notes】caribou: カリブー（北米のトナカイ）, stump: 切り株

■ アツシとコジロウについて、本文の内容に合うものには○を、合わないものには×をつけなさい。
1．はく製の多さに驚いた。
2．恐竜のはく製を見た。
3．エルヴィス・プレスリーの像を見た。
4．よく手入れが行き届いた日本刀を見た。

Scene 2: Paintings of Salvador Dali and John Everett Millais

The painting of Christ of St John of the Cross by Salvador Dali was displayed in a dark room. Christ of St John was looking down at the people from the sky, so we could not see his face. At the bottom of the painting, there was a ship on the blue lake, and some fishermen were working without being aware of St John. The sublime atmosphere of this religious painting overwhelmed Atsushi and Kojiro.

The next section was the corner displaying tartan. Tartan and bagpipes were essential for the people of Scotland. A large red checked fabric and a jacket of an old tartan pattern were exhibited. The explanation and illustrations helped Atsushi and Kojiro to understand the characteristics of the tartan. After this corner, they enjoyed the paintings of Van Gogh, Rembrandt and other great painters.

Atsushi found the painting 'The Ornithologist' on the wall. This was painted by Sir John Everett Millais. He was one of the founders of the Pre-Raphaelite Brotherhood. Atsushi read the explanation of this painting, "In a room an elderly bearded man reclines on a sofa. He holds a stuffed red bird while at his side two children gaze eagerly at the bird, while a young woman leans over him. At the head of the sofa are a boy and a girl and seated at the foot a young girl. To the right are drawers containing specimens of birds and others lie on the covering of the sofa. To the left is a table with a glass globe and an owl." Kojiro fell in love with this painting, because he felt the passion of this intelligent old man.

　Last of all, they dropped in at the museum shop. Christ of St John of the Cross seemed to be the most popular exhibit, because Dali's corner occupied almost all the space in the shop. There they found replica paintings, postcards and books on Dali.

【Notes】Christ of St John: 聖ヨハネ , ornithologist: 鳥類学者

■ 次の質問に答えなさい。

1．ダリの絵画について、簡単に説明しなさい。

　_____

2．ミレーの絵画について、簡単に説明しなさい。

　_____

3．2人は美術館のショップで何を見つけたか。

　_____

● コラム【パディントンのはく製！？】

　本編でアツシとコジロウが様々な動物のはく製があることに驚いているシーンがあるが、イギリス人は希少種を標本にして大事に保存しておくのが心底好きらしい。実際に絶滅した「ドードー鳥」のはく製がロンドンとオックスフォードに現存しており、今となっては貴重な歴史的遺物となっている。そのはく製のおかげで、今では見ることができないドードー鳥がどんな姿をしていたかわかるからである。そこで思い出されるのが、2014年に映画にもなった児童文学作品の『Paddington Bear』である。ペルーの山奥からロンドンにやってきた小熊のパディントンは、心優しいブラウン一家と出会い、彼らと一緒に暮らすことになった。しかし、博物館の研究者から執拗に命を狙われてしまう。パディントンが珍しい種類の熊であるから、はく製にされそうになったのである。なんともイギリス人らしい発想だと、頷いてしまう。

Unit 14

■ Vocabulary Study: Scene 1

1. porcelain　　　　（　）　　a．無料
2. free of charge　（　）　　b．磁器
3. pattern　　　　　（　）　　c．模様

■ Vocabulary Study: Scene 2

1. mounted　（　）　　a．騎士
2. knight　　（　）　　b．騎馬の

Scene 1: Buchanan Street

　Atsushi and Kojiro left Kelvingrove Art Gallery & Museum, and they rode on a City Sightseeing Glasgow bus bound for Buchanan Street. That was the main shopping street in Glasgow. The bus went around the museum, and they could see the beautiful front entrance of the museum. The wide front entrance had a well-kept garden. "That is the main entrance!" Atsushi was

85

surprised at the sight. Kojiro replied, "Did we enter by the back entrance?" It is free of charge to enter most of the art galleries and the museums in the United Kingdom. So, there is more than one entrance to the museum. They looked at each other and laughed.

 Atsushi and Kojiro got off the bus at Buchanan Street. They wanted to take a rest and went into Darcy's cafe. Atsushi ordered a salmon and haddock fish cake and a pot of English tea. Kojiro only selected a cup of hot café latte. The staff brought boiled water in a white porcelain pot covered with a knitted blue and white patterned tea cosy. The knitted pattern might have come from the St. Andrew's Cross of Scotland. After eating the fish cake, Atsushi ordered an apple cherry cake with vanilla ice cream for dessert.

 The two young men had charged their batteries and went shopping in Buchanan Street again. First of all, they visited Whittard. This tea and coffee shop was a branch of the main London shop. Young Walter Whittard opened a small shop in 1886. This shop was known for its unique blends of tea and the rich smell of roasting coffee. Atsushi selected a tin of Scottish Breakfast tea leaves and a tin of biscuits. Next, they went to Hector Russell Kilt Maker's where they selected scarves made of 100% cashmere as souvenirs for their mothers. Kojiro also chose a tartan necktie for himself.

■ アツシとコジロウの行動について、本文の内容に合うものには○を、合わないものには×をつけなさい。
1．2人は博物館の正面を帰り際に初めて見た。
2．カフェで2人は同じものを注文した。
3．カフェでコジロウはデザートも頼んだ。
4．2人とも紅茶とコーヒーを購入した。

Scene 2: Queen Street

Atsushi and Kojiro were walking along Queen Street to buy some food for that night. Suddenly, Atsushi pointed at a statue and cried, "Look at that!" There was a statue of a mounted knight in front of The Gallery of Modern Art. The knight was wearing on his head a red triangular cone which was used at the construction site. In fact, this was an important statue in Glasgow and staff members in the city had removed cones like this one, including traffic cones, again and again. However, each time after they had removed it, a new cone was put on the head of the statue. Finally, Glasgow City Council resigned themselves to the situation and gave up removing the cone. The equestrian Wellington statue with the cone on its head in Glasgow has now become famous. Some tourists took photos of the statue. Needless to say, Atsushi and Kojiro took a picture of the unique statue. "We are lucky to see the statue." "Yes, we can't go back to Japan without seeing this famous tourist spot." They looked deeply satisfied. This statue was the Duke of Wellington, who defeated the army of Napoleon Bonaparte at the Battle of Waterloo.

The two young men found Sainsbury's and bought some food which looked delicious. Among it all, they were curious about Scottish recipe skinless sausages and potato scones, because they had not eaten them before. They went back to their hotel and began to prepare dinner. Kojiro looked over the room and realised that he liked this room in the semi-basement. However, they had to leave there next morning to go back to Japan. He knew that the room was already one memory of the journey. Eating dinner, Atsushi and Kojiro talked about this journey. Scottish people were very kind to them. They were proud of their Scottish spirit, and Atsushi and Kojiro liked that. It was their last night in Glasgow and it was slowly growing late.

■ 本文の内容に合うように、質問に答えなさい。

1．アツシとコジロウが、クイーンストリートで発見したものは何か。

　　_____

2．アツシとコジロウは、ホテルに戻って何の準備を行ったか。

　　_____

3．コジロウは、ホテルの部屋についてどう思ったか。

　　_____

● コラム【ホテルの部屋に冷蔵庫が無い！？】

　グラスゴーで筆者が宿泊した初日、はじめ部屋の中に冷蔵庫を見つけることができなかった。フロントへ行って聞いても「無い」という返事だった。しかし、それでは食材を買ってきても冷やせない。部屋中をくまなく探したところ、薄型テレビの下の戸棚に隠れるように入っていたのを、発見することができた。しかし、見つけた小型冷蔵庫は電源が入っておらず、どうやってコンセントをつなげばよいのかわからなかった。再びフロントへ問い合わせると、「冷蔵庫が部屋にあるはずがない」という不可解なコメントが返って来た。そこで廊下を通りかかった清掃係の女性スタッフに相談すると、親切に部屋に来て問題を解決してくれた。彼女は冷蔵庫を引き出すと戸棚の奥に穴を見つけて、そこからコードを通してコンセントにつないでくれたのである。海外では事に臨む際に簡単に引き下がると、旅行中損をしたり、苦しい境遇で過ごすはめになることもある。交渉をしなくてはならない場合は、度胸を決めて道を切り開いていかなくてはならない。

Unit 15

■ Vocabulary Study: Scene 1
1. barley　　　　　（　）　　a．料理の残り物
2. leftover　　　　（　）　　b．大麦

Scene 1: Back to Glasgow Airport

On the day before going back to Japan, Atsushi and Kojiro finished arranging their luggage. When abroad, tourists had better arrange all their luggage before the day they are leaving. If they overslept, or if they were caught in trouble, they might miss the airplane. If they were prepared, they didn't have to worry.

The two young men woke up at 5:00 a.m. so they could have enough time for breakfast. The leftovers of last night's dinner were warmed up, and they ate them slowly. There were some sausages, a block of cheese, two slices of barley bread, and Greek salad. Besides, a cup of tea and a cup of coffee woke them up completely. They relaxed a while, and then they checked out of the hotel at 6:30 a.m. While Kojiro was carrying the heavy suitcases, a muscular male member of staff came and helped to carry the cases to the entrance of the hotel. The reserved taxi arrived in front of the hotel. The two young men looked up at the deep blue sky, and they rode on in the taxi. They enjoyed looking at the scenery of old-fashioned streets from their taxi window, and arrived at Glasgow Airport at 7:00 a.m.

■ アツシとコジロウについて、本文の内容に合うように、質問に答えなさい。

1．なぜ帰国前日に荷物の整理をしたのか。

_____

2．早朝に起きて何を行ったか。

_____

3．重いスーツケースをどのように運び出したか。

_____

Scene 2: Take off

Atsushi and Kojiro left their suitcases at the check-in counter of the KLM airline. They passed through security inspection and departure formalities. They entered a large duty-free shop to kill time until the boarding time.

There was only 1 hour left. The duty-free shop offered bargain price vodka, Scotch whisky, and other liquors. They wanted to give liquor as a present for Atsushi's father. As a matter of course, they thought that Scotch whisky was the most suitable souvenir for him. They selected a bottle of Bowmore, aged 12 years, that was a single malt Scotch whisky from the Bowmore distillery in Islay. In order to purchase at a duty-free shop, travellers need to show their air tickets. Kojiro knew that rule.

Next, the two young men found a bar & restaurant which had a signboard at the front. There was a picture of a full Scottish breakfast on the signboard. The bacon was fried crisp. Two sausages, a baked tomato, and beans filled up the plate. It looked delicious, but they were not hungry yet, and so they could not try it. Kojiro happened to see a man at the table. He was drinking a pint of beer. It was just 8:00 a.m. Some other people were also drinking beer. This cultural difference surprised Kojiro again.

At 8:35 a.m. there was the announcement for passengers. The two young men went to the boarding gate for Amsterdam. The plane took off at 9:05 a.m. From the window of the plane, Atsushi and Kojiro saw the fields far below. That was a short flight for 2 hours. They had a cup of tea, and fell asleep. They didn't wake up until there was the landing announcement from a captain.

■ アツシとコジロウについて、本文の内容に合うものには○を、合わないものには×をつけなさい。
1．コジロウのお父さんにお土産を買った。
2．美味しそうな朝食の看板を見つけた。
3．朝からビールを飲んでいる人を見つけた。

● コラム【備えあれば憂いなし】

　海外旅行では、帰国前日に荷物をすべて整理しておかなくてはならない。当日、朝寝坊したからといっても、何かアクシデントが起きたからといっても、飛行機は待ってくれないからである。万一乗り遅れた場合は、航空券を買い直さないといけないし、翌日の便に空きがあるかどうかもわからない。その上、一晩余分にホテルに泊まらないといけなくなる。部屋に空きがあるホテルが見つかる保証もない。旅行者は、特に飛行機に乗る日には、予定通りに行動しなければ、大変不都合な目に遭うことになる。だからアツシとコジロウは、朝起きてすぐにホテルを出ることが可能なくらい準備をしてから就寝したのである。

Unit 16

■ Vocabulary Study: Scene 1

1. wake   (　)   a．パエリア
2. the Baltic Sea (　)   b．航跡
3. paella   (　)   c．バルト海

■ Vocabulary Study: Scene 2

1. be relieved (　)   a．次第に
2. gradually   (　)   b．安心する

Scene 1: Long Flight

　Atsushi and Kojiro stayed at the airport in Amsterdam for two hours. This time, they did not go outside the airport. There were various things which attracted them in the shops at the airport. That well-known Dutch product, colourful tulips, were sold in the flower shop. There were many kinds of cheese in the food shop. Looking at a big pile of cheese, they decided to come to Amsterdam again in the future, to eat cheese. Atsushi purchased a tin of waffles for his mother.

At 2:40 p.m. the Boeing 767 jumbo jet took off for Kansai International Airport. Outside the window, the range of red roofs faded from view, and the plane soon flew up high into the blue sky. Kojiro noticed the white wake of a ship in the middle of the ocean far below. Which ocean was it? He operated the panel in front of him so he could see the map. The flight map showed that they were over the Baltic Sea. When the plane was flying over Russia, dinner time came, at last.

Atsushi selected a cup of tea, and Kojiro ordered a cup of coffee. Atsushi chose the Western style menu, and Kojiro selected the Japanese style menu. There was long grain curry paella, and beef curry for the Western style option. In addition, there was a berry mousse and a packet of fruit on his plate. On the other side, on Kojiro's plate, there was Japanese rice, grilled chicken, and grilled salmon with asparagus. Also, Kojiro had gelatin noodles and a rice cake. Both plates had a piece of bread. They ate up the food with pleasure. After dinner, the two young men started using the controller for in-flight entertainment. They wanted to enjoy some movies.

■ アツシとコジロウについて、本文の内容に合うものには○を、合わないものには×をつけなさい。

1．アツシはアムステルダムでお土産を買った。
2．2人はオランダのチーズをたくさん食べた。
3．コジロウはパネルで現在位置を確認した。
4．2人は同じメニューを注文した。

Scene 2: Going back to Japan

The inside of the plane was dark, and most of the passengers seemed to be sleeping. Atsushi and Kojiro had custard ice cream for a midnight snack. Kojiro was watching a movie, but gradually he felt sleepy. He stopped the movie and looked at Atsushi. Atsushi had already put his mask on his mouth and was sound asleep. Kojiro put in his earphones and he selected music. He chose the jazz music and put the volume down. The moderate rhythm of the jazz sent him to sleep. The plane was passing through the night sky of Russia.

There was a wake up sound, and the passengers in the plane were waking up. The aroma of coffee was in the air. The cabin attendants were preparing breakfast for them. Kojiro stretched his arms and checked his watch. It was 6:00 a.m. in Japan. He had already adjusted his watch before going to sleep. He turned on the front panel and saw the flight map. The plane was passing through Beijing in China. It was flying over the Yellow Sea. Atsushi woke up and their breakfasts arrived. The contents were scrambled egg, cucumber and tomato salad, a piece of bread, and a fruit dessert. Kojiro selected a cup of coffee, and Atsushi ordered a cup of green tea. The two young men enjoyed this breakfast very much.

The plane gradually descended to a low altitude. It was 8:00 a.m. and the temperature outside was already 30℃. Until yesterday, the two young men shrank from cold weather. It was not long before the plane touched down on the landing strip of KIX. As soon as the seat belt sign was off, the passengers started to prepare for getting off. The two young men put their jackets into the carry case.

When Atsushi and Kojiro got off the plane, it was very hot and humid. After the entry formalities, they picked up their suitcases without a hitch, and immediately went to the stop for the limousine bus bound for

Nishinomiya station. It was only a few minutes before the departure time. If they missed the bus, they must wait for another 30 minutes. So, they were in a hurry. They got the tickets for the bus, and ran to the bus stop. When they got on the bus and took their seats, they looked at each other and did a happy high five. They were relieved to return to Japan safely. This great journey was one of the most precious experiences for them. However, this was just the start of Atsushi and Kojiro's adventure. The two young men got off the limousine bus with light steps, as if they would soon start their next journey.

■ 本文の内容に合うものには○を、合わないものには×をつけなさい。

1．コジロウは、映画を見ながら寝てしまった。
2．コジロウは、朝食の前に時計を日本時間に戻した。
3．コジロウは、グリーンティーを注文した。
4．日本は蒸し暑かった。
5．アツシとコジロウは、無事に帰国できたことを喜び合った。

● コラム【旅のまとめ】

　スコットランドの旅は、いかがだったでしょうか。楽しんで読んでくれたらと願いつつ、この教科書を執筆しました。
　今や、インターネットで世界中の情報を得られる時代となりましたが、そこから得られるものは、上澄みに過ぎません。実際に現地に行き、そこの空気を吸って自分の足で巡らなければ得られないことは、無数にあるのです。ヨーロッパへ行くと、大都市に必ずといってよいほど大聖堂（カセドラル）が立派なたたずまいを見せています。そこは、いにしえの聖人のお墓であり、その都市の歴史を伝えていることがわかります。また美術館や博物館へ行くと、驚くほど身近で、巨匠の美術品を鑑賞することができます。このように私たちは、実際にその場所を訪れることで、異文化を数多く体験できるのです。
　道がわからなければ、勇気を持って現地の人に尋ねてみましょう。きっと丁寧に教えてくれると思います。マーケットに入り、その土地でどのようなものが食べられているかを聞くのも旅の醍醐味のひとつです。そうやって自分の勇気と語学力で目的を遂げた時の達成感は、何ものにも代えがたいものです。
　いつか海外へ行くチャンスが訪れたときには、是非この教科書の内容を思い出して、少しでも充実した旅にしてほしいと思います。

編集後記

　話がオーストリアのウィーンに飛びますが、この教科書を作るきっかけになったエピソードを記して旅を終わりたいと思います。世界的に名高いケーキ、「ザッハ・トルテ」を知っている人は多いと思います。筆者はホテル・ザッハの1階にあるカフェ・ザッハで本物の「ザッハ・トルテ」を存分に堪能してカフェを出たところ、日本人のツアー団体がカフェ・ザッハの前に現れました。ツアーガイドの日本人女性がザッハについて説明を開始し、説明が終わるとカフェに入るのかと思いきや、驚いたことにツアー団体は去って行きました。最後尾の壮年男性が名残惜しそうにカフェ・ザッハを何度も振り返っていたのが忘れられません。団体旅行のツアーを批判するつもりはありませんが、せっかく目の前まで来たのに、何とも残念ではないだろうかと気の毒に思いました。時間の関係でとても寄ってはいられないのでしょう。

　筆者は若い世代を教育する立場上、若者たちにあの男性のような思いをさせたくないと思い、筆を執った次第です。この教科書は、個人で海外に出る際の手引きを物語風につづったものです。海外に少しでも出てみたいと思う人の一助になれば幸いです。ちなみに、「ザッハ・トルテ」は、意外にチョコの甘みが抑えてあり、しっとりとしたスポンジの食感もよく、間に挟んだあんずのジャムが絶妙の味わいをもたらしていました。

　2015年8月に1週間グラスゴーとエディンバラを訪問し、その時の体験を元にこの教科書を執筆しました。

英文のネイティヴチェックを英文校閲の会社へ依頼したところ、担当して下さった女性が偶然スコットランド在住の方でした。その後、彼女のお嬢さんが2015年8月にヴァイオリンの大道芸をロイヤル・マイルでされていたことがわかり、不思議なご縁を感じました。エディンバラやグラスゴーに精通されている方から、「この二大観光都市についての詳細が非常によく書けていて、光景だけでなく、音や香り、主人公の気持ちの動きまでが生き生きと描写されているので、ワクワクしながら読み進められる楽しい読み物ですね」とコメント頂いた時には、本当にホッとして自信が湧いてきました。

　これからたくさんの学生さんに、英語の力をつけてもらいつつ、スコットランドの魅力、そして旅の楽しさを伝えていけたらと思っています。

著者略歴

福田　範子　ふくだ　のりこ
学歴：神戸女学院大学大学院 文学研究科英文学専攻 博士後期課程修了（2006）
職歴：武庫川女子大学附属中学校・高等学校 非常勤講師（2001-2004）
　　　　　帝塚山大学 非常勤講師（2004-2006）
　　　　　兵庫医療大学 専任講師（2007-2022）
現職：兵庫医科大学 専任講師（2022- 現在に至る）
趣味：美術鑑賞

福田　剛士　ふくだ　たけし
学歴：福井大学大学院工学研究科 博士後期課程修了（2007）
学位：博士（工学）
職歴：大阪大学微生物病研究所 免疫不全疾患研究分野 特任研究員（2007-2011）
現職：鍼灸師・あん摩マッサージ指圧師
資格：鍼灸師・あん摩マッサージ指圧師（厚生労働大臣免許）
　　　　　空手道6段 師範（教士），琉球古武道3段（総合武道 天成道）
趣味：読書

The Great Journey to Scotland

2019年3月31日　第1版　第1刷
2024年3月31日　　　　　第2刷

著　者　　福田範子／福田剛士
発行所　　有限会社二瓶社
　　　　　TEL 03-4531-9766
　　　　　FAX 03-6745-8066
　　　　　郵便振替 00990-6-110314
　　　　　e-mail: info@niheisha.co.jp
装　幀　　株式会社クリエイティブ・コンセプト
装　画　　shutterstock
印刷所　　株式会社シナノ

万一、乱丁・落丁のある場合は購入された書店名を明記のうえ小社までお送りください。送料小社負担にてお取り替え致します。但し、古書店で購入したものについてはお取り替えできません。なお、本書の一部あるいは全部を無断で複写複製することは、法律で認められた場合を除き、著作権の侵害となります。
定価はカバーに表示してあります。

ISBN 978-4-86108-084-5　C3082
Printed in Japan